INSTRUCTION IN CHRISTIAN LOVE

MARTINVS   BVCCER

BVCCER·HAT·VIEL·GVTEN·VN·GLERT
ENGELANT·HAT·ER·AVCH·BEKERT
DAR·IST·BEGRABE·NACH·SEIM·ENDT
AVCH·WIDR·AVSGRABEN·VN·VERBRENT
ABER·DIE·KÖNGIN·LOBESAN·
HAT·DIE·ASCH·EHRLICH·BSTATTEN·LAN

MARTIN BUCER, 1491–1551

Instruction in Christian Love

(1523)

by Martin Bucer, the Reformer

TRANSLATED BY

Paul Traugott Fuhrmann

WITH INTRODUCTION AND NOTES

WIPF & STOCK · Eugene, Oregon

Wipf and Stock Publishers
199 W 8th Ave, Suite 3
Eugene, OR 97401

Instruction in Christian Love [1523]
By Bucer, Martin
ISBN 13: 978-1-60608-100-6
Publication date 7/22/2008
Previously published by John Knox, 1952

To

HENRI STROHL
Christian Historian

and

EDWIN LEWIS
Christian Thinker

"Vulgar happiness consists in receiving, and can never receive enough; love needs to give, and has never given enough; sacrifices exhaust the one, sacrifices sustain the other; and while the first would gain nothing in gaining the whole world, the latter enriches itself by its very losses."

—A. Vinet.

Contents

.

Introduction[1]

Martin Bucer, or Butzer, was born on November 11, 1491, at Schlettstadt—a little city in Alsace yet the seat of a famous school of humanists. Bucer studied at the local Latin School, and at the age of fifteen entered the Order of Preachers or Dominicans. When twenty-five, he was transferred to the Monastery of Heidelberg, where he continued to study theology and the classics, learned Greek under Brenz, and became an ardent admirer of Erasmus.

In 1518 Luther was summoned to appear before the chapter of the Augustinian Order at Heidelberg. The previous year our Wittenberg professor of Bible had asserted that, when Jesus preached repentance, He could not possibly have meant the Roman Catholic Sacrament of Penance. By repentance Luther understood not an institution but an inner state of the soul, a process and movement of our life lasting as long as we live.[2] Such a resurrection of evangelical repentance, the Roman Church authorities felt, would logically displace and even dissolve Penance as her basic institution and chief source not only of donations but also of blessed good deeds. Hence Luther had to come to justify his views at Heidelberg; and thus Bucer had an opportunity to see Luther at this disputation. Bucer undoubtedly heard Luther's twenty-eighth Heidelberg thesis, which in our century turned out to be the fundamental tenet of the Scandinavian reinterpretation of Luther[3]—the thesis which asserts that "Man's love is aroused by what man likes, but God's love finds nothing lovable in man. God creates in man what God loves."[4] Then and there Bucer also heard Luther's strange explanation: "The love of the Cross, born of the Cross, is this: it transfers itself not where it finds some good to be enjoyed, but there where it may confer some good to a sinner or to an unfortunate."[5]

Bucer had also occasion, after the debate, to converse with Luther and to come to know more intimately the original dynamism of the Wittenberg professor. For, according to Dean Strohl,[6] during this personal interview, Luther gave the general outline of his Course on Romans of 1515–1516: "The Christian acknowledges himself as both sinner and righteous at one and the same time: a sinner in reality, yet righteous according to the consideration and sure promise of God, and because of this, he is perfect, whole in hope, though in reality a sinner, but the Christian has the beginning of righteousness, that he may always seek and ask more, always knowing himself unrighteous"[7]—for life, the believer remains at the same time sinner and righteous, always turning to God—*simul peccator et iustus, semper penitens.*[8]

Luther deeply impressed the young Bucer. He wrote to his friend Beatus Rhenanus that "Luther solved all objections, not with the subtlety of Duns Scotus but with the penetration of St. Paul; Luther's concise answers, drawn from the Word of God, astonished everyone . . . Luther very much resembled Erasmus but was superior to him inasmuch as Luther taught openly things which Erasmus had merely insinuated."[9] Bucer professed to have become a "Martinian," that is, to have felt the force of Luther's movement, yet in a sense he remained faithful to Erasmus also. Through life Bucer was indeed a Christian humanist; his ideal was to form complete men:

10

Christians who be cultured, and cultured men who be Christian.

Bucer's further corresponding with Luther, Melanchthon, Spalatin, and Capito, as well as the expression of his new insights, made Bucer's position in the monastery difficult. Hence, having asked and obtained from the Roman See relief from his monastic vows, he joined the secular clergy. He became chaplain of the Palatine Count Frederick, then pastor in the lands of the Knight of Sickingen, in 1522. His ambitious patron, however, having undertaken a war of his own against the Elector of Treves, and lost it, Bucer again had to move. While on his way to Wittenberg, he was retained as a preacher at Wissenburg. He was there hardly six months when the Bishop of Spire excommunicated him on account of his having married; and a new local war forced him to leave again.

Bucer went to Strassburg, arriving there "not as one who had been called but as a fugitive without resources and without position."[10] But he was allowed to remain for two reasons: first, his father had been a Strassburg citizen since 1508; second, the Reformation of Christianity had been at work in Strassburg since 1521—thanks to the statesmanship of James Sturm. Upheld by the magistrate, Matthew Zell, a city priest in sympathy with Luther, had preached new views in the cathedral, and explained in detail St. Paul's letter to the Romans. He had been joined, as canon of St. Thomas Church in Strassburg, by his Alsatian compatriot Capito—a shy man yet a great Hebrew scholar who also was under Luther's spell.

Such was the situation and state of transition when Bucer arrived. Capito's sympathies were with Bucer, but, timid by nature, Capito would hardly do a thing in

Bucer's favor. The episcopal vicary refused Bucer license to preach because of his having married. The magistrate, on the other hand, looked on him with suspicion because of his former association with the rash Knight of Sickingen. But the common people of Strassburg favored Bucer; and, on their instance, he was permitted to offer, in the house of Matthew Zell, a course on the Pastoral Letters. As some persons had asked him to state his faith and to account for it, Bucer wrote this summary of what he would preach[11] and published it under the rather long title of *Das ym selbs niemãt/sonder anderen leben soll. vnd wie der mensch dahyn kummen mög,*[12] which we feel justified in abbreviating and changing into *Instruction in Christian Love—1523.*

The following year, 1524, the Reformation having been officially instituted in Strassburg, Bucer became pastor, first of the St. Aurelia Church, then in 1529 of the St. Thomas Church, and for some twenty years the animating soul of the Strassburg Evangelical Church. His broad liberalism, irenic nature, and humane disposition caused him many sorrows.

Bucer first struggled with the Anabaptists. These emphasized the working of the Holy Spirit beyond Biblical frames, and wished to form congregations of perfect men, while Bucer believed that the Church should take in the multitudes and minister especially to sinners. Yet, while debating matters with the Anabaptists, Bucer absorbed and permanently transmitted into the Reformed Church the concept of the cardinal role of the Holy Spirit.[13]

Another struggle of Bucer was the question of the Lord's Supper which separated Luther and Zwingli, and split early Protestantism. Bucer, holding to the real and mystic presence of Christ in the Eucharist and aiming at the union of Swiss and German Protestants, sought and maintained a mediating position. But he was misunderstood, unsuccessful, and even denounced by both parties. Yet Bucer has truly been the apostle of Protestant unity.[14]

Unfortunate political factors rendered vain Bucer's lifework on the Old Continent. When Protestant and Catholic forces in Germany agreed on a truce, the famous Augsburg *Interim*, 1548, pending a final solution of the religious question, Strassburg was placed in an unfavorable position. Rather than accept the *Interim* or provisory regime which was to bring Romanism back to his city, Bucer left for England whither Archbishop Cranmer had called him, 1549, and, in exile and poverty, died at Cambridge on February 28, 1551. But even his poor body was not to rest in peace. As Queen Mary reintroduced Romanism into England, Bucer's mortal remains were unburied, burned at the stake, and his ashes scattered, 1556.[15]

Yet Bucer still lives. His numerous works remain and may have a future. For, first, Bucer's Biblical Expositions and Christian Treatises are worthy of a careful study because of their mediating the different positions and tendencies within Protestantism. Secondly, Bucer was once and may again become a connecting link between European and Anglo-Saxon Protestantisms. As a thinker, a Christian, and a Cambridge professor, Bucer had indeed great influence on the English Bible, on the Second Prayer Book, and on the person of King Edward VI, for whom Bucer wrote his last great work on the Kingdom of Christ—*De regno Christi*, 1551. Therein Bucer presents the ideal of a nation formed by the Christian Spirit which is to influence and develop all the various aspects of human nature and society. Third and last, the social nature of Bucer's religious thought and activity is worthy to be made known, appreciated, and used in our con-

13

temporary reconstruction of the Protestant vision of life.

The sentiment of Luther was essentially religious, yet in its earliest phase it was connected with ideals of social renovation[16] and economic justice.[17] He at first sympathized with the unprivileged and the oppressed, but on the occasion of the Peasants' Revolt he changed his attitude. Bucer did not start from extremes. His social thought is moderate, stable, and springs from a profound experience of the living Christ and a vivid sense of the reality of the Church. For Bucer, the Church is actually the Body of Christ on earth—that aspect of the Kingdom of God which is at present actual and visible in this world.[18] The Church is the only place where men can become aware of their election and grasp the deliverance which God offers in Jesus Christ.[19] The perpetual question, "Does the authority of Scripture issue from the Church or does the authority of the Church come from Scripture?" had no sense for Bucer. For him, both authorities originate from the living Christ. His Spirit administers the Scriptures and dictates the Church's precepts.[20] Christians, as parts of the Body of Christ, participate in the whole. They share a same spirit, a same vocation, and a same hope.[21]

If some persons think that Protestantism emphasizes the heroism of Faith and neglects the supernatural gift of Charity or Christian Love, this treatise of Bucer shows that this was not the case with the early Protestant Reformers of Christianity.

The reader of this *Instruction in Christian Love,* which is Bucer's very first publication,[22] will here find the earliest social concern of Protestantism and meet the all-encompassing Christian charity of Martin Bucer. His ministry was in fact characterized not only by practical sense but above all by an ardent love for his brethren

14

which made Bucer seek everything that unites and, in the name of our Lord, welcome into the Church anyone seeking Christ with a sincere heart.[23] In no human association is there as much sympathy as in the Church of Christ, for He has freed us from our own selves and gathered us as His own Body so that we may help each other and co-operate to the growth of Christ's Body on this earth.[24]

And now, four hundred years after his death, may Bucer still remind us that God Himself, through His Scriptures, dictates to the state certain duties toward the Kingdom of Christ,[25] and calls us to work and to pray that Christ may really establish His Kingdom among us, guide us toward the life eternal, and reign over us until the end of the world.[26]

The translator wishes to express his gratitude to Dean Henri Strohl of Strassburg for his text[27] and encouragements in life, to Miss Mary Virginia Robinson of John Knox Press, to Professor Ernest Trice Thompson of Union Theological Seminary in Richmond, Virginia, and to President J. McDowell Richards of Columbia Theological Seminary in Decatur, Georgia, for doing their best toward the publication of this precious volume of Bucer.

PAUL TRAUGOTT FUHRMANN

FEBRUARY 28, 1951
FOURTH CENTENNIAL OF
BUCER'S PROMOTION TO
A HIGHER LIFE.

Martin Bucer's Foreword

Martin Bucer to his readers.[28]

May God our Father and our Lord Jesus Christ give you grace[29] and peace.[30] Through our Lord Jesus Christ I thank and highly praise God our Father that He has so kindled in you the love and desire[31] for His Word that you now diligently seek and ask for it. Indeed, righteousness and salvation[32] come to us through the Word which awakens faith.[33] Hence St. Paul rightly calls the Word a power[34] unto salvation[35] to every one who believes in it (Romans 1:16). Since you so eagerly listen to it and so earnestly enquire about it, you are certainly born of God (John 8:47), and constitute a true assembly of Christ. For just as a city which listens to the word of the emperor and keeps his commands belongs to the empire, so the Kingdom of Christ[36] and the true Church[37] are surely where the Word of Christ is heard with such pleasure[38] and observed with such diligence (Isaiah 55:11). As the Word of God cannot return to Him void, but[39] must always capture some, it will not fail among you. The reason[40] for my writing you in the measure of the grace granted me and for offering you my guidance out of our mutual obligation is that some of you, my dear brethren and co-citizens, not satisfied with my sketchy lectures,[41] have asked me to write this little essay. And so according to the Scripture I exhort every one of you not to live for himself, but for his neighbor.[42] I shall later show how to attain this ideal,[43] for it can be realized in this world and life. Since the Kingdom of God consists not of words but of power, may the Father of every grace grant through our Saviour,[44] Jesus Christ, that this perfect state may not remain a matter of mere talk among us. May the Father also make it so that you do not stop at these and other merely human suggestions, but devote yourselves to the divine Scripture and, as loyal sheep of your true and only Shepherd, Jesus, listen to His voice so that you may therewith progress in faith, be perfected in all love, live not at all for yourselves but for your neighbor, and through your neighbor for Christ,[45] and through Christ for the Father Almighty. Praise and glorify Him in eternity. Amen.

Strassburg, August, 1523.

Everyone should live

not for himself

but for others.

How man

may attain this ideal.

FIRST PART: EVERYONE SHOULD LIVE NOT FOR HIMSELF BUT FOR OTHERS

OD has created all things[46] according to His will and purpose (Proverbs 16:4). Hence all things should be directed toward God and be at His service.[47] Anything made is indeed intended to be useful to its maker. Yet a pot cannot by itself help the potter to understand and to speak. Hence, just as objects which man manufactures cannot help man to be man—that is, to exercise his thought and word—so all creatures, not having a character[48] comparable to that of God, cannot help their Creator in divine things. Nothing can help God to be God. Nothing can keep Him from acting as God. Neither, on a human level, can the barrel further the understanding and improve the language of a barrel-maker.[49] However, on a lower level[50] material products such as food—which is not a purely human necessity[51] since we need it in common with the animals—can be useful and even helpful to their producers if the latter throw into a common fund the skills and powers of each by exchanging the products of their hands. Thus the potter sells his pot, and the cooper his barrel; and so each can buy his bread from the baker and his meat from the butcher. Fellowship[52] therefore can really make material things helpful to man.

21

God, however, does not need man's services, because in Himself and by Himself He has and is everything. Being almighty, He can very well do without man. He neither needs nor asks man to help His divine being,[53] which is beyond man's knowledge and comprehension. God's reason for creating us and all creatures is to make His goodness known.[54] He willed that whatever thing exists through His goodness should recognize[55] it and rejoice over it. This is why we His creatures may and should be of service to Him in the administration[56] of His goodness. Namely, each creature, together with its endowments and gifts from God, should serve all others in view of the good of all creatures, to the end that everywhere this praise to God may resound: The Lord is good in all things, and His liberality[57] is over all His works (Psalm 145:9).* And thus, as this same Psalm says, we will speak forth the celebration of His great goodness and joyously proclaim His righteousness (Verse 7).

All creatures are still in this divine order[58] of things —except Satan and man.[59] All other creatures exist, indeed, not for themselves. With all they are, possess, and can do, they serve God in doing good to all other creatures according to their nature and order. The sky moves and shines not for itself but for all other creatures. Likewise the earth produces not for itself but for all other created things. Similarly all the plants and all the animals, by what they are, have, can and actually do, are directed toward usefulness and helpfulness to other creatures and especially to man. For, when God blessed [60] the first human couple, He said to man: "Be fruitful, multiply, fill the earth, subject it, rule over the fish of the sea,

---

* All Scripture quotations are a translation of Bucer's rendering of the original Hebrew and Greek texts.

22

the birds under heaven, and all animals moving on the earth." And God said: "Behold, I gave you every herb bearing seed on the earth, and all trees having by themselves seeds of their kind, in order that they provide food for you as well as for all the animals on the earth, all birds under heaven, and every thing on the earth which moves and has a living soul." And it was altogether so (Genesis 1:28–30).

Those are the words of God. However strange they may seem to us, they must be true.[61] God's word does not consist of mere sounds like ours, but also of acts. He has spoken; and all things were made (Psalm 148:5). As God blessed man, He said to him: "Be fruitful and multiply" (Genesis 1:28). This was not mere talk, but therewith God gave to man the efficiency[62] and power[63] to be fruitful, even the necessity to be so if man does not wish to resist nature. As this alone did not bring forth good, the same God and creator of nature gave man another freedom. That is, God certainly gave man understanding, skill, and power[64] to rule over all other creatures on the earth, in the water, and in the air, and to employ them for his own utility and good. After the blessing[65] of God, it is written: Hence it was altogether so (Genesis 2:1). In order to further secure the submission of all creatures to man, God gathered all the animals and birds before man and let him name them. And what man gave to each as a name became truly its name.

From all this it is clear that all other creatures were meant to subserve man's use. Man was to serve all other creatures in return by using them in the way God had ordained. To use each thing for the purpose for which it was made by God is not only honorable and godly[66] but it brings honor and profit[67] to the thing itself. Examples of this are to wear a suit, to eat bread, to drink

23

wine, to take a wife so that she brings forth children, to seat a wise man in council, and similarly all other things. Yet that there is a service greater than all the services which man owes to all creatures by using them well, God demonstrated by creating for man a being similar to man and planting in this being love for man, with a will to serve him and to do him good. To this degree God willed His creation and creatures to be good and of service not to themselves but to others. Then God also said: "It is not good that man be alone, we will make for him a helper similar to him" (Genesis 2:18). Before, in the first chapter, where God assigned to all creatures their services to man, it is stated that God surveyed all His creation, and it was very good. Without contradiction this passage means that all things are directed one toward the other; all things outside of man are submitted to man so that they may be useful to him. On the other hand, man rules over all things for their own good and usefulness. Consequently all things in their respective order are altogether very good.[68] The Scripture, as a matter of fact, calls good only that which brings good to others, such as a good tree which brings forth good fruits. Speaking properly, God works everything in His creatures and performs the good through them. Only God does good to all things. All other things outside of Him receive more good than they give. Hence Christ could say to the man who called Him good Master: "Why callest thou me good? Only God is good" (Matthew 19:17).

In virtue of the mentioned order, all things were very good. The lower creatures were subservient to man; man used them as he ought to have done, that is, ruled them according to God's decisions and will; creatures were so directed one toward the other that they were mutually useful and doing good one to the other. Thus God performed His goodness through them. As man was meant to live according to the divine image, he had to have also understanding and love for spiritual things like the angels and God. Hence God said: "It is not good that man be alone, that is, that he does not have his like. Otherwise, all things are very good, for they can all be useful to man and do him good, and he can so do to them. But the profit[69] which man brings to other creatures, when he rightly uses them, is yet such that it is altogether only corporeal, that is, on the lower level of bodily things. Now he is to be made so that he might perform also a spiritual service. The other creatures, being merely body, cannot perform this spiritual service. My angels do not need anything. Man, on the other hand, cannot reach us. Therefore we will create another being like man so that, just like us, God the Father, Son, and Holy Spirit, who have in common our divine being[70] and goodness, just like the angels who have associates[71] in a common nature and reciprocal goodness, so man also may have his like whom he is to serve in both spiritual and material things, and to help on both the spiritual and bodily levels, on which man simultaneously exists."

Consequently, in order that man might render such twofold service in a complete way, God created for Adam a companion, a helper similar to man. Before, Adam had many helpers but none like himself. And God planted such a great love in Adam, so strong an eagerness[72] to do good to his companion, that, when the Lord brought him the newly created wife, Adam said: "This is now bone from my bones, and flesh from my flesh. This will be called Manette[73] because she has been taken from the man. Consequently man will leave his father and mother, adhere to his wife, and the two will be as one flesh" (Genesis 2:23). Likewise, by granting to man the power to bring forth fruits, beings of his same nature, and to multiply children resembling him, God has given man further cause[74] to exercise his goodness toward others. Indeed, parents always love their children as their own blood and flesh, and tend in all possible ways to benefit[75] them in both soul and body. Again, a similar affection and desire[76] to do good is planted in children toward their parents; and, since she was created to help him, in the wife toward the husband. If sin had not poisoned nature, such implanted love of one toward the other would never have shown any deficiency in either spiritual or bodily matters. Unhindered by sin, men would have lived without law[77] yet according to the law[78] of God, in friendly service[79] of one toward the other.

But it happened as with the wicked[80] angels. They had been created to be of service to their comrade[81] man and consequently to all creatures. Hebrews 1:14 states indeed that they were all subservient spirits destined to serve those who shall inherit blessedness.[82] But they became transgressors, totally inclined to harm[83] man and set to ruin[84] all creatures; and therefore in turn no longer receive the services of other creatures. As with the damned (Wisdom 5:13), those whom God Himself has abandoned have all creatures against them. That happened also to man when he turned away from God. Thus man has become selfish. He serves only himself and seeks but his own interest. Now man not only does not attain what he seeks, but he has deprived and daily deprives himself of all the benefits and joys which he might and should have from all creatures. For, just as God deals with perverse men according to their perversity (Psalm 18:27), so also all other creatures turn with God against the perverse. According to His nature, God does good abundantly and wishes to make every man blessed[85] (I Timothy 2:4). But if men turn away from God, He must chastise and condemn them; and therein all creatures help their Creator. Because, just as certainly as all things help the good of those who love God (Romans 8:28), so without doubt all things help the decay of those who do not love God. Hence St. Paul speaks: All is pure for the pure, nothing is pure for unbelievers, but both their thought and conscience are impure (Titus 1:15).

Hence it is not surprising that our lordship over all animals is feeble and we so little know how to use the plants of the earth and other creations of God for medicines and other purposes. Today many give huge sums of money for a certain rhubarb and other foreign plants which bring them little help, while they could without cost or trouble find relief in a mess of cabbage—if they knew its virtue.

With the loss of the knowledge of God we have lost also the knowledge of creatures. As we no longer wish to live to serve God, His creatures were rightly taken away from our service. If we ignore the Creator, it is fair that we are deprived also of the created. We have followed Satan[86] and despised God (Romans 1:28 ff.). Hence our whole mind has been perverted to the point that it can no longer be useful to anyone, but rather has become so universally harmful[87] that we have deserved for ourselves eternal condemnation (Romans 1:28–32).

Thus the whole creation, which should have been used only to the praise and glory of its Creator and for the preservation[88] and profit[89] of men, has been disgraced, profaned, and depraved by our diabolical misuse and self-seeking. As far as they can, the godless use creation for the destruction of themselves and others, thus insulting and disgracing God. Hence creation laments and lives in anxiety with all the godly, whom the godless, who

27

fill the world, now mistreat and equally abuse. Subjected to vanity against its will, the whole creation thus waits in expectation and looks for the final manifestation of the children of God (Romans 8:19–22). Since faithless men are void of God, who alone is good, they are void of all good and are nothing but pure vanity, using all things for a vanity which is itself vain. To them the lower creatures consistently are still subjected because God had set man to rule over them. Yet, when the revealing of the children of God shall come—and that shall only happen at the last day—then we shall with Christ be manifested in glory (Colossians 3:4), and we shall be like Him (I John 3:2). Then shall the creatures also become free (St. Paul says) from serving corrupt existence, in order to share the glorious freedom of the children of God (Romans 8:21). The whole creation shall again contribute to man's good and blessedness;[90] man will then rule over nature, using it to the glory of God; and God will be all in all (I Corinthians 15:28). When the created shall again stand in its original order, when each creature shall be directed to the other for its utility, joy, and blessedness, then God, with His elect (the condemned shall have no part in it),[91] will again look with favor at His creatures, at the entire creation, which, as in the beginning, shall be very good. Henceforth the eternal work of creatures and the elect[92] shall be to maintain by their praises the celebration of the great goodness and righteousness of God (Psalm 145:7).

From all this it is clear that no one should live for himself, because God created all things[93] so that they might contribute not to their own good but to that of others, and be an instrument and evidence[94] of the divine goodness which all things should express and spread forth. The Lord God had first established this order of things at the time of creation. God will again bring it about at the time of the renovation of the world,[95] when God will entirely do away with sin, which has broken the primeval order, and will again bring in His Kingdom.[96] Of all bodily creatures, only man is created after the image of God in order that he may understand and also choose spiritual things, and thereby grasp, follow, and fulfill the will of God. He requires us to desire to further the profit[97] and salvation[98] of all. Hence, before all creatures, man must[99] so direct his being[100] that in all his doings he seeks not his own, but only the welfare[101] of his neighbors and brethren for the honor of God. Thereby man will also use well and rightly all other creatures and blessedly rule them for their own welfare and proper honor.

This is clearly shown by what the Lord says: "All that which you wish people to do to you, that do to them also; this is the Law[102] and the Prophets" (Matthew 7:12). By nature and custom we are so minded that we wish every man to do us good, and no man to do us evil. If we used the same standard toward every other man, doing him good, we would put our life in that right order to which the Law and the Prophets point. Were we able to do that, we would already be perfect and have fulfilled the whole Law. Hence St. Paul speaks: All the laws[103] would be accomplished in one single word which is, Love thy neighbor as much as thyself (Galatians 5:14). Everyone knows how every man loves himself. If a man, however, wishes to follow Christ, that is, to be turned around and brought again in his right standing and character,[104] he must take all that love which poisoned nature had him place on himself, and put it all on his neighbor.[105] For love, which is the fulfillment of the Law, seeks not itself but always the profit and welfare of others (I Corinthians

13:5)—be they friends or enemies.[106] This is emphasized in all Scripture, especially John 13 and 15, Romans 14, I Corinthians 10 and 13, Philippians 2, and the entire letter of John. It is well that the duty of love be wider toward comrades[107] in faith (Galatians 6:10 and further passages), since they are receptive of spiritual benefits, teaching, exhortations, and warnings through the Word of God. Yet one must make no difference between men— whoever and however they are—but have the same love and desire to procure for each all the good to which he is responsive (Matthew 5:43 ff.).

From this it follows that the best, the most perfect and blessed condition on earth is that in which a man can most usefully and profitably serve his neighbor. However, as spiritual service is superior to material service, and as the community is more important than particular individuals, the ministry of an apostle is the most accomplished office, vocation, and service. The ministry serves not some particular men, but the community; it deals not with material but with spiritual things, and leads to eternal blessedness. Such a ministry consists in this—that the one who is thereto called and ordained by God, dedicates himself to serve God the Father and our Saviour Christ in the work of making the sinner blessed. According to I Timothy 2:4, this was the unique office of our Lord and Saviour[108] Jesus Christ. The minister therefore willingly stakes[109] not only his body and sacrifices not only his material possessions but also his spiritual life and blessedness, if only his preaching the divine Word would lead others to a knowledge of God, to blessedness, and thereby to praise and eternally to glorify the goodness of God. Moses was so minded. When the people of Israel had sinned, he begged God to forgive them, and said: "Lord, either forgive this sin of the people or erase

30

me from the book which thou hast written" (Exodus 32: 32). Likewise Paul writes: I tell the truth in Christ Jesus and I lie not, my conscience is my witness in the Holy Spirit, I have in my heart a great sadness and a restless affliction: I have desired to be banished from Christ for the sake of my brethren (Romans 9:1–3).

This should be the mind of all popes,[110] bishops, and spiritual leaders if they wished to be held as the representatives of Christ and successors of the Apostles. Thus Christ has not only put up His soul and bodily life for us His little sheep (John 10:11), but was also cursed for our sake so that we might have a part in the blessing of Abraham (Galatians 3:13–14). He, who knew no sin, for our sake became sin so that in Him we might become that righteousness which is valid before God (II Corinthians 5:21). God has burdened Him with all our unrighteousness; and He bore it with joy (Isaiah 53:4–5). In this, as expected, His true disciples and apostles followed Him. They not only withstood all dangers and material privations for the good of believers, but they cheerfully accepted being held as sinners, cursed and damned people, on account of their brethren. As the Epistle to the Romans showed us above, they desired to be so cursed and banished provided their brethren would obtain blessedness. That damnation, however, is just as impossible as the retention of Christ by death (Acts 2:24). For God said to Moses (when he begged to be taken off the Lord's book if God willed not to forgive the people of Israel): "Him who sins against me, will I erase from my book" (Exodus 32:33).

He commits no sin, therefore, who loves God and desires to please Him to such an extent that he is ready to forfeit his own salvation[111] in order to obtain this blessedness for his neighbors. Just as with Paul, neither life nor death, neither angel nor domination nor power, neither thing present nor thing future, neither height nor depth nor any other creature, could cut him off from the love of God in Christ Jesus our Lord (Romans 8:38–39). Nothing could banish Paul from Christ. The love of God in Christ Jesus was so great in him that, just as Christ had given Himself for the sins of others, so Paul in turn—though he could not possibly be cut off from that love—desired (and earnest desire often wishes the impossible) to be banished from Christ if only Paul could thereby bring many to God and increase the divine glory.[112] Not that Paul wished to fall from the love of Christ, but, on the contrary, on account of the greatness of this love he wished to be stripped of Christ's grace and blessing provided these could be transferred to his brethren. Paul, who had learned to value himself less than anyone else (Philippians 2:4, 17), wished that, instead of himself alone, many others would come to know Christ, to glorify and to praise God for eternity. And this he calls that carrying the burden of others which accomplishes the law of Christ (Galatians 6:2). Although we should all so do, one toward the other, this conduct befits[113] especially those who watch over us in place of the Apostles, those who represent the office of Christ, who are His foremost servants and the stewards of the mysteries of God (I Corinthians 4:1). Hence Paul writes the Philippians to see to it that those who exercise this ministry take him as an example (Philippians 3:17). Moreover, Paul diligently exhorts Timothy and Titus to offer to believers such a pattern.

Hence, with the greatest diligence, pray to God that all those who claim apostolic dignities, and occupy the places not only of the Apostles but also of Christ—that is, our churchmen, bishops, and spiritual leaders—may not depart too much from the example of Christ and the Apostles. If they cannot yet attain that perfection in love which would dispose them to sacrifice their blessedness for that of their neighbors and subordinates, may they at least, without seeking shameful personal profits and vain honors, impart[114] to them faithfully the Gospel and see to it that it be communicated[115] to them. May they draw near a little and have a bit of that apostolic disposition[116] which the Law, the Prophets, Christ, and all the Apostles set forth. It is St. Paul, however, who in all his Epistles and especially in I Thessalonians 2, expresses that feeling[117] most clearly. It cannot be denied that most churchmen, as one may sadly see, now everywhere seek their own interest and not the benefit and blessedness of those under them, except in the measure in which the others' benefit and blessedness bring them material advantages and subserve their prestige. Their behavior is quite contrary to the apostolic office and to Christian sentiment.[118] *Hence, churchmen have fallen from their highest and most worthy standing, from the all-divine function of which they were proud and which they enjoyed.*[119] And so they now lie on the lowest, most despised, most diabolical level characterized by an utterly cursed and anti-Christian way of life.[120] They are just like Satan, whom God had once dignified far above all men, and who now is rejected and damned below all damned men. The office of those churchmen required of them to be with Christ and, through a faithful preaching of the Gospel and without seeking their own advantage, to gather believers. The moment they began to relax, it followed that, as Matthew 12:30 states, they turned against Christ and scattered. As the present conditions sadly show, those who, only because of the Gospel, are so richly entertained and are mighty lords in this world, not only do not preach the

Gospel but do all they can in order that it be not preached and heard. This will to drag others with oneself to eternal damnation is certainly a satanic undertaking. From all this it is evident that at present there is no more dangerous, more disquieting, and more condemnable condition than that of churchmen, popes, bishops, clergymen,[121] and monks. Because, according to the names and status which they have taken, they ought to employ all their diligence to promote the common good and spiritual betterment, and thereon to stake[122] their possessions, their bodies, their honor, their happiness, seeking in nothing their own interests. In reality they not only leave all this aside, but with all their doing and not-doing, with all their words and works, they are a hindrance to the common good. And with all earnestness they aim at oppressing[123] all those ecclesiastics who faithfully preach the Gospel. Hence, watch out for the above class of men and their way of life[124]—if it is possible for you. And withdraw from it—if you can.

Though its office is not concerned directly with spiritual things such as preaching the Word of God, the estate nearest to the ministry is that of secular authority.[125] It consists in keeping good order and outer peace, in protecting the godly,[126] and, by its penalties, in keeping the ungodly from wronging the godly. The service of the civil authorities is such that it reaches the whole community, whose welfare it should procure by maintaining the common peace and law. This is much more than being at the service of particular businesses and individual men of the community. After the office of pastors,[127] which is faithfully to provide the community with the Word of God, the office of the secular authority,[128] or magistracy,[129] is the most deserving. This public office requires men who also completely deny themselves and seek nothing for

34

themselves. For selfishness in private affairs hinders a man from acting in a responsible[130] and Christian way toward his neighbor. And without that love which seeks not its own (I Corinthians 13:5), no activity or deed[131] can be Christian and of good report.[132] Selfish authorities hinder even more the honorable and Christian management[133] of the whole community. Even the pagan Aristotle[134] drew the difference between a good ruler and a tyrant by saying that the ruler seeks only the welfare of his subjects while the tyrant seeks his own. So Homer[135] wished that a king[136] would not sleep all night because of his concern for his subjects. Homer would not leave a moment to the king in which to look after his own interest.

Although the service which secular authorities owe to the community does not consist in preaching the divine Word and Law, yet civil officials must[137] govern[138] according to the Word of God and, in the measure of their power, help the success of the divine Word. For as there is no power[139] which is not from God, and everywhere the present powers[140] are established by Him (Romans 13:1), it certainly follows that this power[141] must be exercised according to the order and will of God. Only so will this power[142] at last procure the real welfare[143] of its subjects and thus stimulate them to recognize,[144] praise, and glorify God as the Lord of all lords and the King of all kings. But the citizens are not governed for their good and for the true glory of the supreme King when the secular authorities[145] do not rule according to the divine Law and are not set to observe it themselves. For where God is not recognized[146] and obedience to Him is not required before all things, there peace is not peace, justice[147] is not justice,[148] and that which should be profitable brings injury[149] instead.

God therefore forbade the people of Israel to get from foreign people a king[150] who would not be a brother, and commanded the people to accept as king him whom the Lord would elect from their brethren. The king was to write God's Law and to read it all the days of his life so that he might learn to fear God his Lord, to keep His word and the injunctions of the Law,[151] neither to raise his heart in pride above his brethren nor to deviate either to the right or to the left (Deuteronomy 17:15-20). If a man, therefore, is to govern beneficially and not to be a tyrant, it is necessary that he be elected by God and from among the people of God. That is to say, he must be a true believer who has not himself stepped forward for the office but has been called to it.[152] The Christian official, recognizing himself as undershepherd of sheep which are not his own but God's, thinks to govern them not as it seems good to him but according to the Law of God to whom the sheep belong. Consequently a civil officer should day by day govern and treat the people of God according to the divine Law.[153] In great humility and constant awe, he stands before God in order to avoid the least mistake in executing such a great commission.[154]

This Solomon observed. He asked God to give him a teachable heart before all things, so that he might judge his people and know the difference between good and evil (I Kings 3:9). In this prayer he professes that he had been placed above God's people and not above a people belonging to Solomon himself (I Kings 3:8), to judge it, to lead it to good, and to keep it from evil. He also confesses that human reason[155] has not the power of distinguishing between evil and the true good, of judging rightly, but needs to learn such things from God. Thus enlightened, we can well recognize[156] the heavy divine plague with which God has plagued us and which comes

36

from the fact that we call ourselves Christians and consider ourselves the people of God, and yet our officials who have the power[157] have fallen into the error[158] of believing that the divine Law[159] does not concern them, that they must judge and make regulations more according to the pagan imperial law[160] and other human sentences than according to the sentence of God. In this they show themselves bailiffs of men and not of God, since they govern their subjects according to the sentences of men and not according to the divine pronouncement. Now, anywhere a man whose law[161] is observed is recognized as lord. No one on earth would consider as belonging to the German emperor a city which would direct all its affairs and regime[162] according to the commands and prohibitions of the French king, and completely ignore the imperial law.[163] Consequently, we cannot pride ourselves on being communities of God and the people of God, if[164] we respect, accept, and keep all sorts of laws, ordinances, and regulations other than God's. Only His Law can make us live.

We must declare that just as God infinitely goes beyond all human wisdom and prudence, so the ordinance and sentences of God go beyond all the laws, organizations, and governments which men have devised, passed, and established in order to enforce honesty and make peace secure. Whence comes our perverted unwillingness not only to heed but even to hear the ordinances of God, and our mocking those men who remind us of them? If someone in a council or legislature were to refer to the divine law which demands the death penalty for adultery [Leviticus 20:10], what laughter he would get! The same honor would go to any who according to the Law of God should suggest penalties toward the abolition of prostitution, the preaching first of all the Word of God to the

37

people, and the death penalty for all those who falsify or hinder it. According to the divine Law such are indeed the obligations of a Christian magistrate and official, as godly princes and kings like Moses, Joshua, David, Hezekiah, and others have shown.

But, sadly, many civil officials act as if they were not bound by their oath, which is not only to men but also to God. In their administration they pay no attention to the divine sentence and often act intentionally against it. Thus they decide nothing in the interest of the community, unless of course they see at the same time a chance to increase their prestige and fortune. And it happens also as with the aforesaid churchmen. The higher they rise the more positions they accumulate, but they do not exercise the beneficial responsibilities of their several offices. On the other hand, the lower they fall the more despicable their character becomes through misuse of their high power.[165] And so more and more they harm the community over which they preside. Hence, just as those negligent and inefficient churchmen were condemned to become apostles of the antichrist instead of apostles of Christ, and devils instead of angels, so our civic lords and leaders—who ought to be shepherds and fathers, that is, lieutenants of God—have become nothing but lions, bears, wolves, children,[166] and jackanapes. As Solomon says, A godless leader ruling over a poor people is like a roaring lion and a hungry bear (Proverbs 28: 15).[167] We read of such leaders[168] in Ezekiel 22:27: The princes in the midst of the land are like wolves devouring their prey; they shed blood, destroy[169] the souls, and out of greed they seek dishonest gain.[170]

Let us blame our sin for our having false apostles instead of Apostles, and seducers for teachers.[171] Let us blame also our godless character for our having tyrants,

38

wolves, bears, lions, babes, and fools instead of pious and God-minded leaders and civil authorities—as Isaiah 3 and Hosea 13, leaving aside several other pages of the Scripture, clearly inform us. Every day, moreover, experience shows that if[172] the godless rule, and the people lament (Proverbs 29:2), yet the heart of the king and certainly the heart of all authorities is also in the hand of the Lord, who can turn it wherever He wishes. Hence we must first of all, as St. Paul teaches, offer prayers, supplications, and thanksgiving for the authorities (I Timothy 2:1), so that God according to His heart may give us shepherds and leaders as His own officers ruling us according to His Law, and further our obedience to His commandments. For just as in both spiritual and secular things all our profit and welfare depend on our leaders faithfully attending[173] to their office, so also our whole ruin without doubt comes from their seeking their own advantage and making us obey themselves and not God.

God established these two general orders, the spiritual ministry and the secular authority, in order to further the public good.[174] They could perceptibly bring it about if they attended to their commission, but they could also irreparably injure[175] it if they sought only their own interest. Below the aforesaid two orders are the most Christian orders or professions. They are agriculture, cattle-raising, and the necessary occupations therewith connected. These professions are the most profitable to the neighbors and cause them the least trouble.[176] Every man should encourage his child to enter these professions because children should be encouraged to enter the best profession, and the best profession is the one which brings most profit to neighbors. But nowadays most men want their children to become clergymen. In the present circumstances, this means to lead a child into the most dangerous and godless position. The rest of men wish their children to become businessmen always with the idea[177] that they would become rich without working, against the commandment of God (Genesis 3:19), and with the idea that they will seek their own profit while exploiting and ruining others,[178] against the divine order and the whole Christian spirit.[179] Encouraging youth to enter that road is leading them to eternal death, while the path to eternal life is only through keeping the divine commandments. And all commandments will be fulfilled in the single injunction of brotherly love, which always seeks the interest of the neighbor and not its own.

To conclude, this first part should have made it clear:

that, according to the order and commandment of the Creator, no one should live for himself but each man should out of love for God live for his neighbor and by all means[180] be of service to him in matters pertaining to both the spirit and the body;

that this obligation rests above all on those who were called and established to promote public utility, both spiritual and secular;

that God could not send us a greater plague than men seeking their own advantage;

that the more a profession is useful to the needs of the general neighborhood and furthering the profit of the whole community, the more that profession is honorable and Christian and should be cheerfully entered or accepted by each.

Finally, our first part shows that we live now in the last times,[181] in which injustice has taken the upper hand and love has become extinguished (Matthew 24:12); each man seeks and conforms to the easy life and wishes to live on the work of others, while the Christian life demands exactly the opposite. The Christian gives up even what is rightly[182] due to him, is always ready to help others by his work, and accepts nothing for nothing, holding on to the words of Jesus: It is more blessed to give than to receive (Acts 20:35).

SECOND PART: HOW MAN MAY ATTAIN THE IDEAL OF LIVING NOT FOR HIMSELF BUT FOR OTHERS

OW it must be said how we may return to such a life as that for which we were first created, that is, living not for our own benefit but for that of others, and for the glory of God. To put it briefly, only Faith can bring and impart such a life to us. All things indeed have been created through Christ Jesus our Saviour. Therefore it pleased[183] God through Him also to bring all things again into the position and order in which they had at first been created. God's revealing of His true children (Romans 8:19), that is, the advent of men who are true believers, would benefit the other creatures (Isaiah 11:6). From men, then, must begin this universal return to the earliest and right character[184] of creatures. Though not yet perfect, this return of men must begin here and now. And that will happen if men believe in Christ, namely, fully trust that by His blood Christ has placed them again in the sonship and grace of the Father and that consequently by His Spirit Christ has also remade them according to the earliest world order, that is, useful to many and understanding all creatures. This restoration will reach each man according to his degree of receptivity and responsiveness.

For Christ is to each man and does for each man according to that man's trust. He said to the blind men (Matthew 9:28): "Do you believe that I can do such a thing for you?" And they spoke: "Yes, Lord." He then said: "Let it be so to you according to your faith." But we have through our sin fallen from our first estate, in which we lived to serve others and to praise God. And now—a sad thing to say—according to our poisoned nature we love only ourselves and seek only our profit. Thereby we now ruin ourselves, hurt our neighbor, insult God, and disgrace our Creator. But we must believe that God, by making our Lord Christ head of His community (Colossians 1:18), has reconciled and united all things through Him (Ephesians 1:10); that is, God has brought all things back to their original character[185]— living for the glory of God and usefulness to all creatures, but especially to men. Yes, we must believe that this restoration through Christ, this reconciliation and reorganization through Christ, reaches us also. Then the spirit of true love will certainly return to us—that spirit which is considerate in all things and seeks not its own but the welfare of the neighbor. For His word must hold: It will be to you according to your faith.

Further, true faith can make it so that we completely believe all the words of God—the whole Scripture which pictures unto us Christ Jesus our Saviour[186] as Him who by His blood has rescued us from the power[187] of darkness and through the grace of the Father has placed us in His Kingdom (Colossians 1:13). Consequently now we are not only free but also true children of God. For, if we believe in His name, He has given us the power[188] to become children of God (John 1:12). The Father indeed sent into our hearts His Spirit which cries: Abba—dear Father. So now there are no longer slaves but only children. But children are also heirs, heirs of God through Christ (Galatians 4:6). The same Paul writes also to the Romans (8:14-17): It is therefore clear that through faith we become children of God and have the spirit of children, which makes our spirits sure that we are children of God. It must follow as a consequence that just as through the Spirit we recognize[189] and call on God as a father, so we also recognize[190] all men as our brethren and place ourselves at their service. This especially pleases the Father because He had created us for this purpose, which He has pointed out to us by means of all His Law and Prophets.[191] Only faith can therefore detach us from ourselves and make us give ourselves over to God the Father as children. When we have thus become true children, our highest concern must be to follow the will of this dearest and best of fathers and in all things to live according to His Law. And all this is fulfilled if we follow this single word: Love thy neighbor as much as thou lovest thyself. As soon as we yield in this to the Father, we completely give ourselves to the service of all men for the joy and glory of our heavenly and dearest of all fathers.

This is easy for all those who have true faith. Because, as we saw, faith brings with itself the spirit of children, the Spirit of God which witnesses to our spirit that we are children of God. If we are children, then we are also heirs —heirs of God and co-heirs with Christ. If we acknowledge and hold ourselves as children and heirs of God and believe ourselves such with certainty (and nothing is more certain than that we believe on the word of God) we must also acknowledge and hold as the most certain thing of all that we possess and shall receive all necessary things. Yes, we must consider ourselves as nothing else than already blessed,[192] although now only in hope, since we shall receive God's eternal inheritance only on the day

44

in which we shall with Christ appear in the glory of God and be like God (Colossians 3:3-4; I John 3:2).[193] For just as little as a good and faithful father, who is in a position to help, can leave his dear children in want, so much the less will our eternal Father let us suffer want. He knows and can do all things; and does the best that a father can do for his children. Hence what the prophet[194] says is certainly true: Those who fear God lack nothing (Psalm 34:9). These are, however, only the dear children of God through faith.

Our nature is so attached and subservient to worldly goods, and is always so anxious to get enough of them, that it has no free will to help others unless it has first helped itself with what it imagines to be indispensable. But our nature will never rest from helping itself and never believe that it has gained enough. Only the certainty of being children and heirs of God can give the security of already possessing what is necessary for both the present and the future. Only true faith can put the heart at peace. Then the heart recognizes with certainty that it shall lack nothing. Then the heart thinks like Paul: If God has not spared His own Son but has given Him for us all, how could He not give us all things beside? (Romans 8:32). The meaning is: If God has sacrificed for us what was most dear and precious to Him, His only and beloved Son, which sin of ours will He not overlook? What good could He withhold from us? His love is too great. Hence as soon as, through faith, the heart recognizes[195] and holds this truth, so soon the heart is overflowed with love and thereby completely made ready to do good to all men, and eager first of all, by proclaiming to them the unspeakable goodness of God, to lead them to this blessed sense of security. For the nature of true goodness is such that it cannot keep to itself but must pour itself out as far and as wide as possible. No good tree can be without fruit, and good fruit besides (Matthew 7:17-20).

Faith not only brings into us a complete trust in Christ but it also restores us to that right and divine order in which we had been created. Moreover, through faith we are offered and accept His Spirit which makes us certain that we are children of God. As a result we gladly do all kinds of deeds of love for our neighbor. These acts of service and compliance are God's highest demands on His children. Inasmuch as we are children, heirs of God and ourselves blessed—namely, certain that we shall suffer neither present nor future want—we feel the further need to serve our brethren in all faithfulness and with that unfeigned love which springs from faith. As we learn from the Scripture, by nature we are children of wrath[196] (Ephesians 2:3), and hence unworthy to be served by anyone; but[197] the Lord has promised[198] us that He will accept as done unto Him what we do for the least of His brethren (Matthew 25:40), and He will let lovingkindness[199] thrive in all those who practice it toward their neighbor (Matthew 5:7). For the Lord demands lovingkindness[200] and not offering (Hosea 6:6). All this should cause us heartily to rejoice[201] that serving and showing our neighbor all tender consideration[202] is required of us, for thereby we are allowed to show a little gratitude to our most gracious Father and Saviour[203] and with confident hearts to expect from Him wider lovingkindness[204] since we now apply ourselves—a little at least—to do His will.

Further, since only faith recognizes and rightly appreciates the immeasurable benefits of our Lord and Redeemer[205] Jesus Christ, faith constantly recalls them for an ever new celebration and keeps those benefits in ever fresher meditation. Hence it must follow that the man who has faith[206] shall acquire the same disposition which he sees Christ to have possessed (Philippians 2:5). Namely, though existing in altogether divine form, Christ did not consider this similarity to God as a prey, but He stripped Himself, took the form of a servant, became like any man, still further humbled Himself and became obedient even to death, yes, to the death on the cross (Philippians 2:6-8). If a believing heart meditates upon that, it shall be so kindled to love for his Saviour[207] and Lord that it will completely renounce itself, strip itself, and think: If the eternal Son of God, thy Saviour[208] and Lord, has not come to be served but to serve others, if He has given His soul for thee and the deliverance[209] of many, if He stripped Himself of the divine form in which He was, if He took the form of a servant, if He has become obedient even in death, and the death on the cross, what then wilt thou, O man, do with thyself? Oh, may I, at least a little, follow my Lord and Deliverer[210] as a token of my gratitude, I who am nothing and can do nothing. All I have is through Thee out of the grace of the Father. I will keep nothing for myself but with joy will put all I possess at the service of my brethren. I will also be obedient in death, even in the death of the cross; that is, I will accept all sufferings and disgrace. And so it will happen that we shall deny ourselves, put the cross on our shoulders and thus follow our Lord, Master, King, and Saviour[211] (Luke 9:23), and certainly also like Him pass from this life of humility, service, and obedience into the eternal glory, kingdom, and blessedness. Amen.[212]

Faith, finally, takes away from us love for the present life—its honors, fortune, and pleasures—love which hinders so many from exercising a true love and service to their neighbor.[213] Yes, true faith frees us from all that,

47

Because through Christ faith shows the heavenly and eternal Father so gracious toward us, so ready to pour all goods upon us, that material things are now a vexation and a burden for the believer, who would gladly leave everything in order to be with Christ (Philippians 1:23), where he would also be free from sin and no longer offer cause to displease[214] his very dear heavenly Father. Consequently the believer considers this present life and all its demands more as a burden than as a great good. Hence, without mentioning honors, possessions, or pleasures, giving his life for his brethren is a small matter for a true believer. Thus Christ in His endless love toward us has given even His life for us (John 3:16).

These but brief indications yet suffice to show that only faith brings us back into our primeval right and godly disposition[215] as God had first created it, to His praise, so that we may be useful and of service to all creatures—seeking in nothing our own interest, for which our Father and Creator, God the Almighty, has already provided. Faith is true righteousness in which the righteous man at last lives as he should live toward God, man, and all creatures (Habakkuk 2:4).[216] He gives to God the honor and praise due to Him, and practices toward his neighbor that love which fulfills all commandments (Galatians 5:14). Thus we show ourselves disciples of Christ, keeping His new commandment (John 13:34), and through it all the Law and the Prophets. Thus we show that we shall certainly pass from this Christian godly life into the eternal life.

And here many may as well learn what kind of faith is theirs. For faith brings self-denial, dedication of self to the service of other men, forgetfulness of self and[217] living wholly for others to the glory of God. If faith is not such, then it is not true and legitimate faith, it is a dead faith, it is no faith at all.[218] If faith brings forth the above fruits but weakly and imperfectly, then faith, too, is weak and imperfect. It is a sad thing to say, but, with a few exceptions, such is the faith of most of us. For if faith were whole, complete, if the heart were giving itself completely to the Scripture, and this in all earnestness, and not believing only illusions,[219] it would be impossible for man to seek his own or to live only for himself, because he would certainly and precisely know from the Scripture that by such self-seeking he would destroy himself, lose his life and everything (Luke 9:24; John 12:25).[220] Hence out of necessity he must give himself with his whole heart and trust to that unspeakable goodness which the Scripture describes as ready for him in God the Father and which is given to him through Christ as soon as he has faith. And through faith he is wholly renewed. Henceforth he can no longer care about himself, for he is assured that the eternal God, his Father, cares [221] for him as for His dear child. And [222] the believer, like a perpetual spring, must pour out the goodness which God imparts to him through Christ by furthering the welfare of all men, yet especially of his comrades [223] in faith. For the latter are quick to receive not only material goods like other men but spiritual benefits as well.

By way of conclusion, I wish again to show with a saying of St. Paul that a man who has true faith has become altogether other than he was, that in Christ he is a new creature who no longer can live selfishly, but must live for the advantage of his neighbor and to the glory of God. This word of St. Paul is clear. He says: By grace you have been saved; [224] and that not of yourselves. It is the gift of God, not because of works, in order that no man may pride himself on them. For you are His work, created through Jesus Christ for good works, for which God has in advance prepared us so that we may walk in them (Ephesians 2:8-10). We can see how clearly this saying states that if we believe, we are through faith blessed,[225] that is, assured of all the necessary things. This does not happen because of ourselves and our own good deeds, but simply by our accepting everything as a gift of God's grace. We are indeed the work of God, created through Jesus Christ for the accomplishment of good deeds. We are not, however, to perform these acts for our own benefit but simply because God in advance has prepared us for them so that they shall be our way of life.[226]

These works are, without doubt, those which God everywhere commands us, namely, those by which we serve our neighbors. God demands no other works from us; and Christ has taught us no others. Hence He so often quoted the saying of Hosea 6:6, I want lovingkindness and not the offering, and declared[227] that He will judge us accordingly (Matthew 25). If a believer is a work of God, created for performing such good deeds, he certainly cannot remain idle or seek and do good only to himself. For what God has created through Christ Jesus must be good, right, and under obligation to apply itself to[228] that for which it has been created just as all the other works and creatures of God attend to[229] that for which they have been created. The bird attends to flying, the fish to swimming, and man to speaking. Just as little as any creature or work of God can disregard that for which it has been created, unless an accident occurs, so little can a Christian and true believer live without doing good works, forgetting himself, benefiting all men, doing and giving to each according to his ability to receive and to respond.

By now it has been clearly enough shown that true faith is that through which we come to live not for ourselves but for others to the glory of God, and to be assiduous in truly good works. Hence it can also be seen that to preach faith is to point out the spring of all good deeds, while nothing is farther from our thought and proclamation than forbidding good works. Finally, we must also pay attention to this: If we are negligent in accomplishing the good deeds in question we certainly have little faith. If we perform no deeds and remain self-seeking, we have no faith at all. And I Corinthians 13:1-13 states: If we spoke with the tongues of men and even angels, if we told the future, knew[230] all mysteries and all science,[231] yes, even if we had such a colossal faith so as to transpose mountains, that is, if we had the drive[232] of faith which is the gift of working miracles—a gift at times lent to those who have otherwise no true faith in God, as it is clearly shown in those who, though having wrought miracles in the name of the Lord, yet shall hear Him say, "I have never known you" (Matthew 7:22)—if we had distributed all our possessions to the poor and even given our body to be burned, yet we would be nothing if we had no love. So it is of all those who seek nothing but their own interest, for love seeks no advantage. We also are nothing if[233] we have no faith, for through faith we are not only made something but are blessed,[234] as the passage above emphasizes. As a matter of fact, we are a work of God, who is not only something but certainly something good.

As true faith surely brings true love which makes us overflow with good works toward our neighbor,[235] and live not for ourselves but for the eternal glory of God, and as faith comes from God's grace through hearing the Word of God (Romans 10:17), we must above all things adhere to the divine Word, hear it, read it, meditate on it with all diligence, and act accordingly. We must let no man keep us from the Word of God; for it we must risk honor, life, possessions, and all that which God has given us. For only the Word of God makes us wholesome and blessed. The divine Word brings faith; faith brings love; love brings good deeds as its fruits—after which God gives us the eternal inheritance, a wholly divine and blessed life. Amen.[236]

Notes

NOTES ON INTRODUCTION

1. J. W. Baum, *Capito und Butzer*, Elberfeld, 1860; A. Courvoisier, *Bucer*, in *Encyclopédie des Sciences Religieuses* edited by F. Lichtenberger (Paris, 1877), Vol. II, pp. 458-459; C. Crivelli, *Bucero*, in *Enciclopedia Cattolica* (Vatican City, 1949),Vol. III, cols. 166-167; Schenkel, *Bucer*, in *Real-Encyklopädie* edited by Herzog (Stuttgart and Hamburg, 1854), Vol. II, pp. 412-423, were consulted, as well as the other works which will be found in the notes following.

2. *Dominus et magister noster Jesus Christus, dicendo: Poenitentiam agite etc. omnem vitam fidelium poenitentiam esse voluit. Quod verbum de poenitentia sacramentali, id est confessionis et satisfactionis, quae sacerdotum ministerio celebratur, non potest intelligi*—are the first two of Luther's 95 Theses, 1517, *D. Martini Lutheri OPERA LATINA varii argumenti* (Frankfurt and Erlangen, 1865), Vol. I, p. 285; Luther's Works (Philadelphia, 1943), Vol. I, p. 29. See Henry E. Jacobs, *Martin Luther* (New York and London, 1898), p. 72; Félix Kuhn, *Luther—Sa Vie et Son Oeuvre* (Paris, 1883), Vol. I, pp. 211, note, 236, 265, and our note 236.

3. Cf. Edgar M. Carlson, *The Reinterpretation of Luther* (Philadelphia, 1948).

4. *Amor Dei non invenit, sed creat suum diligibile, amor hominis fit a suo diligibili, D. M. Lutheri op. cit.,* p. 403.

5. *Et iste amor crucis ex cruce natus, qui illuc sese transfert, non ubi invenit bonum, quo fruatur, sed ubi bonum conferat malo et egeno, D. M. Lutheri op. cit.,* p. 404.

6. H. Strohl, *Bucer, humaniste chrétien* (Paris, 1939), pp. 6, 26; H. Strohl (ed. and transl.) in Martin Bucer, *Traité de l'Amour du Prochain* (Paris, 1949), pp. 6-7, 41 n.8.

7. *Simul peccator et iustus; peccator re vera, sed iustus ex reputatione et prommissione dei certa . . . Ac per hoc sanus perfecte est in spe, in re autem peccator, sed initium habens iustitiae,*

53

ut amplius querat semper, semper iniustum se sciens, *Luthers Vorlesung über den Römerbrief: 1515-1516,* ed. by Johannes Ficker (Leipzig, 1908), Vol. II, p. 108.

8. *Ibid.,* pp. 266-267. Luther uses also longer phrases, as *semper partim peccatores, partim iusti, i.e. semper penitentes, ibidem,* p. 267. See also our notes 2 and 236.

9. In Felix Kuhn, *Luther—Sa Vie et Son Oeuvre* (Paris, 1883), Vol. I, p. 233; Johann Wilhelm Baum, *Capito und Butzer* (Elberfeld, 1860), pp. 96-97; and *Luther's Correspondence and Other Contemporary Letters,* Translated and Edited by Preserved Smith (Philadelphia, 1913), Vol. I (1507-1521), pp. 80-82.

10. Gustav Anrich, *Martin Bucer* (Strassburg, 1914), p. 18, quoted by J. Courvoisier, *La Notion d'Église chez Bucer dans son développement historique* (Paris, 1933), pp. 3-4. This latter book is far more comprehensive than its title suggests, being really on the thought of Bucer as a whole.

11. H. Strohl in his edition of Bucer's *Traité,* p. 5.

12. Literally: That no one should live for himself but for others, and how man can come therein (i.e., attain that ideal). In his edition of this treatise, note at page 7, Dean Strohl suggests that this title of Bucer's may have been inspired by the concluding paragraph (30) of Luther's *Christian Liberty.* There Luther says: *Ausz dem allen folget der beschluss / das eyn Christen mensch lebt nit ynn yhm selb/sondern ynn Christo vñ seynem nehstenn / ynn Christo durch den glauben/ ym nehsten/durch die liebe:* "From all this the conclusion follows that a Christian man lives not in himself but in Christ and in his neighbor: in Christ through faith, in his neighbor through love." *Luthers Werke in Auswahl,* ed. by Otto Clemen (Bonn, 1912), Vol. II, p. 27; Luther's Works (Philadelphia, 1943), Vol. II, p. 342.

13. J. Courvoisier, *op. cit.,* p. 8.

14. John T. McNeill, *Unitive Protestantism*—A Study in Our Religious Resources (New York, 1930), pp. 21, 56, 77-78, 109, 137, 146, 149-162, 164-168, 175, 180-185, 195-196, 228, 238, 244, 254.

15. Constanin Hopf, *Martin Bucer and the English Reformation* (Oxford, 1946), and additional information in its review by Dean Strohl in *Revue d'Histoire et de Philosophie Religieuses,* 1950, No. 2, pp. 141-145.

16. The early sermons of Luther (cf. e.g. *Opera Latina varii argu-*

menti, Vol. I, pp. 25-226) have a social element, especially those on the Lord's Supper.

17. Compare his elemental catechism of 1520, the *kurze Form: Ich glaub das in diszer gemeyne odder Christenheit/ alle ding gemeyn seynd / vund eyns yglichen güter des andern eygen / vnd niemant ichts eygen sey, Luthers Werke in Auswahl*, ed. by Otto Clemen (Bonn, 1912), Vol. II, p. 51. Luther's Works (Philadelphia, 1943), Vol. II, p. 273. (In Reformation times, German capitalization and spelling were irregular. Luther's Latin at times has *e* instead of *ae*, and *i* instead of *j*.)

18. Bucer, Expositions of St. Paul's Letters, Vol. I: *ad Romanos*, (1536), p. 19, quoted by J. Courvoisier, *op. cit.*, p. 94; see also pp. 56, 69. J. Courvoisier published also *Une traduction française du Commentaire de Bucer sur l'Évangile selon saint Matthieu* (1540) extracts concerning the Law, holydays, the Sacraments, and the Church (Paris, 1933).

19. Bucer, *De regno Christi*, French translation (Geneva, 1558), p. 47, in J. Courvoisier, *La Notion d'Église chez Bucer*, p. 121.

20. J. Courvoisier, *op. cit.*, p. 92.

21. J. Courvoisier, *op. cit.*, p. 98.

22. According to an annotation of Bucer's secretary (Conrad Hubert) on the title page of the copy preserved at Strassburg Divinity School, reproduced in facsimile in *Traité*, p. 14. Cf. also H. Strohl, *ibid.*, p. 5, and J. W. Baum, *op. cit.*, p. 589.

23. J. Courvoisier, *op. cit.*, p. 80.

24. Bucer, *ad Romanos*, p. 462, quoted by J. Courvoisier, *op. cit.*, p. 87.

25. Bucer, *Grund und Ursach*, 1524, O III b; *De regno Christi*, French translation (Geneva, 1558), p. 189 in J. Courvoisier, *op. cit.*, p. 131.

26. Bucer, *Von der wahren Seelsorge*, 1538, c X IIII b in J. Courvoisier, *op. cit.*, p. 115.

27. Martin Bucer, *Traité de l'Amour du Prochain* [original German text with], *traduction, introduction et notes par* Henri Strohl (Paris, 1949). The translator here wishes to thank Dean Strohl for his four publications (1922-1934) on Luther which first encouraged him to study the Reformers.

NOTES ON BUCER'S FOREWORD

28. Literally, "hearers."

29. *Gnad* from *nah,* near, like the Latin *propitius* from *prope,* near. Ancient Germans said *die Sonne geht zu Gnaden,* meaning, the sun goes down or approaches the horizon. *Gnade* thus originally meant approach by descending, hence literally condescension, then it came to mean favor shown to an inferior. In 1523 spelling and capitalization were neither consistent nor uniform.

30. German, *frid.* "The Hebrew language has this characteristic, that while the Latin said *Valere, bene habere,* the Hebrew says 'to have peace.' Hence the greeting in the Gospel is in the Hebrew wise: *Pax vobis,* Peace be with you."—Luther, Exposition of Psalm Thirty-seven (Wittenberg, 1521), on verse 37. And Spinoza will say: Peace is not absence of war, but a virtue which springs from the soul's strength.

31. German, *begyrd* (or the verb *begehren*) is stronger than mere *wunsch* or *wünschen,* for it implies earnest effort. It is related to the Old English *giernan,* to yearn.

32. German, *heil* (cf. the Old English "hale," robust, vigorous, especially in old age). This literally meant health (cf. the English "whole"). Cf. note 44 on *heyland.*

33. Literally, "the word and faith."

34. *Krafft* means power in the sense of efficacy, efficiency. A medicine may have *Stärke,* or be strong, and yet have no *Krafft,* efficacy. Cf. notes 63, on *Macht,* and 139, on *gewalt,* for different meanings of "power."

35. German, *heil.* See note 32.

36. In Bucer's thought *das reich Christi* is a reality. Literally *Reich,* from the verb *reichen,* to extend, refers to extension of territory and power. See note 37.

37. German, *kirch,* church. The word was first coined in Gothic and then passed into the German language, where it still survives. In Bucer's mind, the Church is not only the Body of Christ but also the inner core of the Kingdom of Christ and the irradiating center of Christ's influence in this world.

38. German, *lust,* pleasure, desire. The English word "lust" once meant the same. *Lust* and *list* are related and once were the

56

same word. Listless still means "without pleasure or desire."

39. German, *sonder* (but), was originally a verb, like the English "to sunder." It forcefully marks an antithesis or contrast.

40. German, *vrsach,* cause. Literally it means "original" (*ur*)— "thing" (*sache*) and hence fitly designates a cause.

41. On the Pastoral Epistles, and delivered at the home of Matthew Zell.

42. German, *nechsten. Nechste,* neighbor, is simply the superlative of *nah,* near. The reader will notice that Bucer so often uses the singular (neighbor). Christian Love (supernatural gift of God through the Holy Spirit) is not sentimentally spread over anonymous masses but is focused on our single, definite neighbor.

43. German, *stand der volkummenheit,* state of perfection.

44. German, *heyland.* A participle of the Old German *heilan,* modern *heilen,* to heal. For another word meaning "savior," cf. note 205, on *erloeser.*

45. An allusion to Matthew 25:31–46, according to H. Strohl, in *Traité,* p. 9, note 1. Bucer refers to this passage at p. 50 and quotes it twice in another treatise, that is, in the *Summary seiner Predig* (also of 1523), pp. 63, 71, and in almost all his writings. Also Luther (in his exposition of Luke 16:23–24) and Farel (in his *Summaire* of 1525) spoke of and loved this grandiose apocalyptic scene which is simply the counterpart of the Beatitudes. Here at the end (as indicated in the passage from Matthew), the promises of Jesus are shown to be realized. The obscure men, whom Jesus addressed and who followed Him in history, here surround the Son of Man in glory and judgment, and are admitted into God's Kingdom. Notice the singular noun (neighbor) in Bucer's text. (See note 42.)

NOTES ON THE FIRST PART OF BUCER'S INSTRUCTION

46. German, *alle ding*. *Ding* includes whatever is created, is, or exists. *Sache*, "thing," is included under *Ding* but it excludes persons, while *Ding* includes them. *Sache* is generally "object of human pursuit, occupation, or interest." *Personen und Sachen* (not, *Personen und Dinge*) would make a contrast. God is the creator of all *Dinge* (not only *Sachen*).

47. German, *dienstlich*, subservient.

48. German, *wesen*. This is an old infinitive (equivalent to *seyn*) used as a substantive. Its simplest meaning is "being," character of a person or of a thing. It also means essence (in philosophy), difficulty, disturbance, affair (e.g., *Kirchen-Wesen*: the Church affairs).

49. Was Bucer thinking of his father who was a cooper?

50. German, *haendeln*: activity, affairs. *Handel* once meant action of any sort. It then came to mean affair, business, trade.

51. German, *haendeln*. See note 50.

52. German, *gemeynschafft*, from *gemeyn*, common, collective. (Cf. note 17.) The word conveys a more elemental concept than *Gesellschaft* (from *sal*, hall), society.

53. German, *wesen*. See note 48.

54. From *erkennen*. *Kennen* means to know in the sense of "to distinguish or recognize." *Kennen* has usually to do with what the eye (physical or spiritual) can see. *Wissen* means to have knowledge of, and has to do with acts of the mind.

55. From *erkennen*. See note 54.

56. German, *Regiment*: control, government, administration, from *regieren*, for which see note 138.

57. German, *miltiggkeit* (and *milthätigkeit*) from *milde*: free, liberal, abundant, beneficent.

58. German, *wesen*, here in the sense of order. Cf. *Das gemein Wesen*: the commonwealth; *Das Staats Wesen*: the state.

59. Cf. a page similar to this in Luther's *Magnificat*, 1520–1521, in Clemen's ed. *cit.*, Vol. II, p. 154; Luther's Works (Philadelphia, 1930), Vol. III, pp. 153–154.

60. Old German, *gebenedeyet,* from the Latin *benedicere.* Its opposite was once *maledeien* from the Latin *maledicere.*
61. Here Bucer's original text has in its margin: "God's speech."
62. German, *Krafft.* See note 34.
63. German, *Macht,* might. Cf. note 34 on *Krafft,* and note 139 on *Gewalt.*
64. German, *Macht.* See note 63.
65. German, *segen,* benediction, act of blessing, is a corruption of the Latin *signum,* sign. When Christianity was introduced into Germany, as the sign of the cross was made in benediction, the sign itself was confused with the benediction or blessing. The same is true of the verb *segnen* from the Latin *signare,* to make a sign—the sign of the cross in our case. In very ancient German, *segen* is found in its original meaning of *signum* and *vexillum.*
66. German, *frummen. Frumm* originally meant profitable, helping the interest of. This sense remains in the verb *frommen.* As an adjective, it came to mean good, pious, godly. As a noun it means advantage.
67. German, *frummen.* See note 66.
68. Here the original text has in margin: "What is good."
69. German, *frummen.* See note 66.
70. German, *wesen.* See note 48.
71. German, *genossen,* from *geniessen,* to enjoy, means an associate in something pleasing. It is a deeper term than *Gesell* (from *sal,* hall), associate in business, and *Gefährte,* traveling companion.
72. German, *begyrd.* See note 31.
73. German, *Maennin,* woman of the man.
74. German, *vrsach.* See note 40.
75. German, *frummen.* See note 66.
76. German, *begyrd.* See note 31.
77. German, *gesatz.* This was once simply the participle of the verb *setzen,* and meant simply "settled, established." As a substantive, it came to mean the law. The English word "law" once meant simply "laid": that which is laid down.
78. German, *gesatz.* See note 77.
79. German, *in freüntlichem dyenst.* For *freünt,* cf. note 106.
80. German, *boesen.* The adjective *boese* indicates something evil in itself. It is the opposite of *gut,* good. *Uebel,* evil, implies rather injury, doing wrong. Its opposite is *wohl,* agreeable.
81. German, *mitgenossen.* See note 71.

82. German, *saeligkeit,* from *sal,* a hall or large lower room in ancient German houses, hence possession of goods therein; or from Old German *sael,* that is, *heil,* hence possession of *heil,* for which see note 32. *Saeligkeit* is the possession and enjoyment of the grand total of spiritual goods.

83. German, *schaden,* to injure, whence the Anglo-Saxon *scathan,* whence the English "scathe" with a narrower meaning.

84. German, *verderben,* to render unfit for use.

85. German, *selig.* See note 82.

86. German, *der teuffel,* the devil. Both words are a corruption of the same Greek word *diabolos,* slanderer.

87. German, *schaden.* See note 83.

88. German, *heil.* See note 32.

89. German, *frummen.* See note 66.

90. German, *saeligkeit.* See note 82.

91. The belief in election is not popular. Yet the American people elect only a few men to their Congress. Jesus believed in election: Mark 13:20, 22, 27 (Matthew 24:22, 24, 31), Luke 18:7. Luther, Zwingli, and Bucer believed in election or predestination. They drew this conviction not from philosophy but from the Scripture and from personal experience (that so many men are utterly blind to the Gospel).

92. German, *erwoelten,* the elect. See note 91.

93. German, *alle ding.* See note 46.

94. German, *instrument,* tool, document having legal value. Tertullian used the word *instrumentum* in the latter sense, with reference to the Scriptures. Cf. his *Adversus Hermogenem,* 19, 20; *De resurrectione carnis,* 33, 39, 40, and *Adversus Marcionem,* 2.

95. Matthew 19:28; 25:31–46; Acts 3:21; Revelation 21:1, 5.

96. At present we have the Kingdom of Christ. The perfect Kingdom of God is only at the end. Cf. Matthew 25:31–46; I Corinthians 15; and notes 36, 37, 45, and 95.

97. German, *frummen.* See note 66.

98. German, *heil.* See note 32.

99. German, *gebürt,* it belongs to, in the sense of "it is due from."

100. German, *wesen.* See note 48.

101. German, *wolfart,* a prosperous course of things. Both the German *fahren* and the English "fare" originally meant simply to go, as in "farewell." But the verb came to be applied to any process of life or business.

102. German, *gesatz*. See note 77.

103. Bucer here has the plural (*gesaetz*), not the singular (*gesatz*).

104. German, *wesen*. See note 48.

105. German, *nechsten*. See note 42.

106. German, *feynd oder freünd*. *Feind*, enemy, is simply the present participle of *fian*, to hate, and means a bitter, malignant enemy, hence (like the English "fiend") the word was often applied to Satan. *Freünd*, friend, from the Old German *frijon*, to love.

107. German, *genossen*. See note 71.

108. German, *heyland*. See note 44.

109. German, *in die schantz schlagen*, to throw in an entrenchment. Cf. Mark 8:35.

110. German, *Baepst. Bapst*, like the English word "pope," comes from the Late Greek *papas* or *pappas*, which meant father. The name was reserved for the pope. A local priest or spiritual teacher was called *Pfaff*, for which see note 121.

111. German, *heil*. See note 32.

112. Such views on self-denial are found already in Tauler, and in the *Theologia Germanica* edited by Luther in 1516 as well as in his Course on Romans of 1515–1516, mentioned at notes 7 and 8, Vol. II, pp. 215, 217–218. Dean Strohl notes that Bucer may have heard them from Luther himself as he met him at Heidelberg. See also our note 5 and our corresponding page 10.

113. German, *gebürt*. See note 99.

114. German, *mitheylten*. *Theil*, part, is the same word as the Old English "deal"—a part. "To deal" once meant to divide—like the German *theilen*.

115. See note 114.

116. German, *gemuet*, meaning the disposition, the feeling. It corresponds to the Latin *animus, sensus*. Cf. the English "mood," frame of mind. Before Shakespeare, the English word "moody" meant courageous, high-spirited, stubborn.

117. See note 116.

118. See note 116.

119. The italics indicate Bucer's emphasis.

120. German, *wesen*. See note 48.

121. *Pfaffen*, from *papa*, priest, was first coined in Gothic, and thence passed into the German language. It was once used in addressing church teachers and priests. During the Reformation, it ceased to be an honorable title. Since then, *Pfarrer* (from *Pfarre*, parish, and *Herr*, sir), pastor, is used in addressing clergy-

men. Luther uses both *Pfaffen* and *Pfarrherren* in his Address to the German Nobility, 1520. Cf. O. Clemen's ed. *cit.*, Vol. I, pp. 362–425; Luther's Works (Philadelphia, 1943), Vol. II, pp. 61–164.

122. German, *daran setzen:* thereon to wager, to risk.
123. German, *verdrucken.* In Bucer's time *verdrucken* meant to oppress, as *be-* or *unter-drücken* means now.
124. German *wesen.* See note 48.
125. German, *weltlicher oberkeit,* the civic magistrates. Also in 1523, Luther published the treatise *Von weltlicher Obrigkeit.* (Spelling and capitalization were not uniform in 1523.) Cf. O. Clemen's ed. *cit.*, Vol. II, pp. 360–394; Luther's Works (Philadelphia, 1930), Vol. III, pp. 228–273.
126. German, *frummen.* See note 66.
127. The *Geistlicher* is a general term embracing bishops, secular clergy, and religious orders.
128. See note 125.
129. The original text has in margin, *Ampt weltlicher regierer.* (Office of secular government.) For *regierer.,* see note 138.
130. German, *redlich,* from *Rede,* account. It meant "of good report," proper. Today it generally means "honest."
131. German, *haendeln.* See note 50.
132. See note 130.
133. See note 56.
134. Aristotle's Politics (Book IV, Ch. 10) in Desiderius Erasmus, *The Education of a Christian Prince,* translated by Lester K. Born (New York, 1936), p. 161. The original Latin text (Basel, 1516) was known by Bucer.
135. In D. Erasmus, *op. cit.,* p. 184.
136. German, *Künig* (like the English "king"), probably from *künne,* race, means of noble race. Tacitus wrote that the Germans chose their kings from the nobility: *Reges ex nobilitate sumunt.*
137. German, *gebürt.* See note 99.
138. German, *regieren,* to rule, to administer—from the French *régir* or Latin *regere.*
139. German, *gewalt* (from *walten,* kindred with the English "wield," to control), the legal power involving superiority and ability to compel.
140. See note 139.
141. *Ibid.*
142. *Ibid.*

143. German, *wolfart*. See note 101.
144. From *erkennen*. See note 54.
145. See note 125.
146. See note 54.
147. The German *recht* corresponds to the Latin *jus:* conformity to the laws, the right, justice.
148. See note 147.
149. See note 83.
150. See note 136.
151. See note 77.
152. D. Erasmus, *op. cit.*, p. 160.
153. *Ibid.*, p. 167.
154. German, *befelch. Befehl* now means command, but in Reformation times it meant to commit. Luther says *ich befehle meinen Geist in deine Hande.*
155. German, *vernunfft*, reason. It corresponds to the Latin *ratio. Geist* is the Latin *mens.*
156. From *erkennen*. See note 54.
157. German, *gewalt*. See note 139.
158. The original text has in margin: "Note this, secular judges."
159. See note 147.
160. *Ibid.*
161. German, *gesatz*. See note 77.
162. See note 56.
163. Our reader will recall that, at the time of Bucer, Strassburg was in the boundaries of the German Empire, and will see here a good *argumentum ad hominem:* Bucer takes advantage of the situation of the Strassburgians in order to make his point clear and to convince them that they should accept the Law of the Lord.
164. German, *so*, which, in common with the Old English, often meant "if."
165. German, *gewalt*. See note 139.
166. See Isaiah 3:4.
167. D. Erasmus, *op. cit.*, p. 167.
168. German, *Fürsten. Furst*, being simply the superlative of *für*, the old form of *vor*, meant the foremost, the first, and hence the leader—like the Latin *princeps*, and the English "prince."
169. German, *verderben*, to render unfit for use.
170. D. Erasmus, *op. cit.*, p. 167.
171. The italics indicate Bucer's emphasis.

172. German, *so,* which often meant "if."
173. The German *warten* originally meant to look, to look for. Hence *warte* meant an elevated spot, a tower on which to look out, an observatory. *Warthurm* and *Wartburg* meant watchtower. The verb, therefore, meant to watch, to wait anxiously for, and, like the English "wait on," came to mean also attending to, taking care of.
174. Cf. a page similar to this in Luther's *Magnificat,* 1520–1521, in Clemen's ed. *cit.,* Vol. II, p. 134 (cf. pp. 186–187); Luther's Works (Philadelphia, 1930), Vol. III, p. 124 (cf. p. 200).
175. German, *schaden,* to injure. See note 83.
176. The text of 1523 has here in margin: "Christian standings" (orders).
177. German, *meynung,* from *meinen:* low German *meenen* (English "mean"), purposing.
178. Dean Strohl observes that similar ideas had already been expressed in ch. 73 of the famous *Narrenschiff* (Strassburg, 1520), *folios* 144–145. Cf. *The Ship of Fools,* by Sebastian Brant, translated into rhyming couplets and edited by Edwin H. Zeydel (New York, 1944). Experience, however, led Bucer to modify his views in favor of businessmen, this especially in his last book, *De regno Christi.*
179. German, *wesen.* See note 48.
180. German, *krefften.* See note 34 on *krafft.*
181. Such was also the conviction of Luther. This fact is persistently ignored, though so conservative a scholar as Julius Köstlin had to acknowledge it already in 1881. See page 531 of his *Life of Luther* (New York, 1913). For the early expectations and views of Luther (c. 1517–1522) see the present translator's article, The Three Kingdoms According to Luther, in *The Lutheran Outlook,* Vol. XVI, No. 6, June 1951, pp. 173–176, or his pamphlet with notes, Luther's Vision of the Kingdom of God (Westminster, Md., 1951).
182. i.e., legally: *von recht.*

NOTES ON THE SECOND PART OF BUCER'S INSTRUCTION

183. German, *hat gott gefallen:* God has pleased. *Fallen,* to fall, at the root of the word gives the impression of an unforeseen and sudden occurrence or decision of God.
184. German, *wesen.* See note 48.
185. *Ibid.*
186. German, *heyland.* See note 44.
187. German, *gewalt.* See note 139.
188. *Ibid.*
189. From *erkennen.* See note 54.
190. *Ibid.*
191. Our reader, recalling the expression *weisen mit den Fingern,* will think with Bucer that the Law and the Prophets are the great forefinger of God pointing out man's true destiny. See p. 29.
192. German, *selig.* Cf. note 82.
193. See notes 95 and 96.
194. Luther, Farel, and later Calvin, throughout his *Institution* of 1541, also refer to or quote the psalms as "the prophet."
195. German, *erkennt.* See note 54.
196. German, *Zorn:* fiery passion, just anger or righteous indignation —not to be confused with fury *(Grimm)* and rage *(Wuth).*
197. German, *sonder.* See note 39.
198. The German *verheissen* properly meant to make a declaration or promise to an inferior, since *heissen* was used about or applied to a superior giving directions to an inferior.
199. The German *barmhertzigkeit* corresponds to the Latin *misericordia.* Both involve and have at their center the heart *(Hertz, cor).*
200. *Ibid.*
201. The German verb *freüwen* means to experience a feeling of pleasure *(Freude)* arising from a loved object for whose sake suffering is not excluded. Being thus joyful *(freudig)* is something deeper than being *lustig* (sportive) or *frölich* (joyous) with reference to external manifestation.

202. See note 199.
203. German, *heyland*. See note 44.
204. See note 199.
205. German, *erloeser*. From *erloesen,* which means literally to make one loose from something that held him, to free one by the exertion of power or with effort. Next it means to redeem, i.e., to purchase one's freedom.
206. Literally, the believing man.
207. German, *heyland*. See note 44.
208. *Ibid.*
209. German, *erloesung.* See note 205.
210. *Ibid.*
211. See note 44.
212. Dean Strohl suggests that this passage may have been inspired by paragraphs 26 and 27 of Luther's Christian Liberty. *Luther's Werke in Auswahl,* edited by Otto Clemen (Bonn, 1912), Vol. II, pp. 24–25; Luther's Works (Philadelphia, 1943), Vol. II, pp. 335–338.
213. Again Bucer uses the singular, indicating that love is not scattered over the masses but is concentrated on the single neighbor.
214. German, *erzürnen,* to irritate, to anger. Verb related to *Zorn.* Cf. note 196.
215. German, *wesen.* See note 48.
216. For Luther, faith was a state, almost an entity: only when men are *in* Faith, can they understand the Law of God. See his Exposition of Psalm Thirty-seven (Wittenberg, 1521), on verse 31. For Luther, God's Word also was (one could say) a metaphysical entity. Hence Luther could say: "We must make a great difference between the Word of God and the word of man. The word of man is a light sound which goes up into the air and soon vanishes, but the Word of God is greater than heaven and earth, even greater than death and hell, for it is the Power of God and will remain eternally; hence we must apply ourselves to study the Word of God, and believe and know with certainty that God himself speaks to us." Luther, *Propos de Table,* translated by G. Brunet (Paris, 1844), p. 193.
217. See note 39.
218. The original text has here in margin: "Imperfect faith." This passage of Bucer reflects the typical ideas of Luther on faith as the source of love and Christian activity.

66

219. German, *won*, whim, illusion.
220. See note 218.
221. Note the contrast: man's care (worry) and God's care (providence).
222. German, *sonder* (but), in contrast with man's former self-centeredness. See note 39.
223. See note 71.
224. German, *selig*. See note 82.
225. *Ibid*.
226. Literally, "so that we should walk in them." Here the German *wandern* is—like the English—to walk, in the Biblical sense of a course of life.
227. See note 198.
228. German, *gewarten*. See *warten*, note 173.
229. *Ibid*.
230. German, *wisten*. See *wissen*, note 54.
231. Old German, *erkantnüsz*, knowledge. See *erkennen*, note 54.
232. German, *tryb*.
233. German, *so*, which often meant "if."
234. German, *selig*. See note 82.
235. Cf. Philip Melanchthon, the *Loci Communes*, Translation and Critical Introduction by Charles L. Hill (Boston, 1944), pp. 202–204. For Luther, see our observation in note 218.
236. Bucer's original text had this final paragraph: "Hence, in these perilous times in which faith declines and love is sadly extinct because the divine Word has not been faithfully and diligently preached, we must with all earnestness pray God that He may send us a rain of His pure divine Word, give us the grace of accepting it, and either convert or otherwise bring to an end those who so senselessly withstand Him. Amen." The editors place this final paragraph in the notes because it would, in the text itself, seem strange to the average reader (whom Luther used to call Mr. Everybody), who has no experience of the opposition faced by Bucer. For our English "convert" in the paragraph placed here, the German original text has *beker*, which meant to turn about in the opposite direction. Simply to turn in general would be *wenden*. The German *Bekehren* exactly corresponds to the Semitic *shub* used by the Prophets, John the Baptist, and our Lord Jesus. Cf. F. Delitzsch's and Salkinson-Ginsburg's Hebrew Testaments. The great contribution of the Reformers was their rediscovery of the concept of Biblical re-

pentance, not as the mere Semitic *tohu* (regret), nor as *harat* (remorse), nor as *charatah* (sorrowful change of mind), nor as *niham* (regretting, feeling sorry), but as the positive, even joyful, *teshubah:* returning (to God) as a way and course of life. See our notes 2 and 8. On the prophetic nature of early Protestantism, see J. Calvin, *Instruction in Faith* (Philadelphia and London, 1949), pp. 7, 8, 10, and p. 95, note 241.

Nunc dimittis servum Tuum, Domine,
secundum Verbum Tuum in Pace.

THE END

29666831R00042

Printed in Great Britain
by Amazon